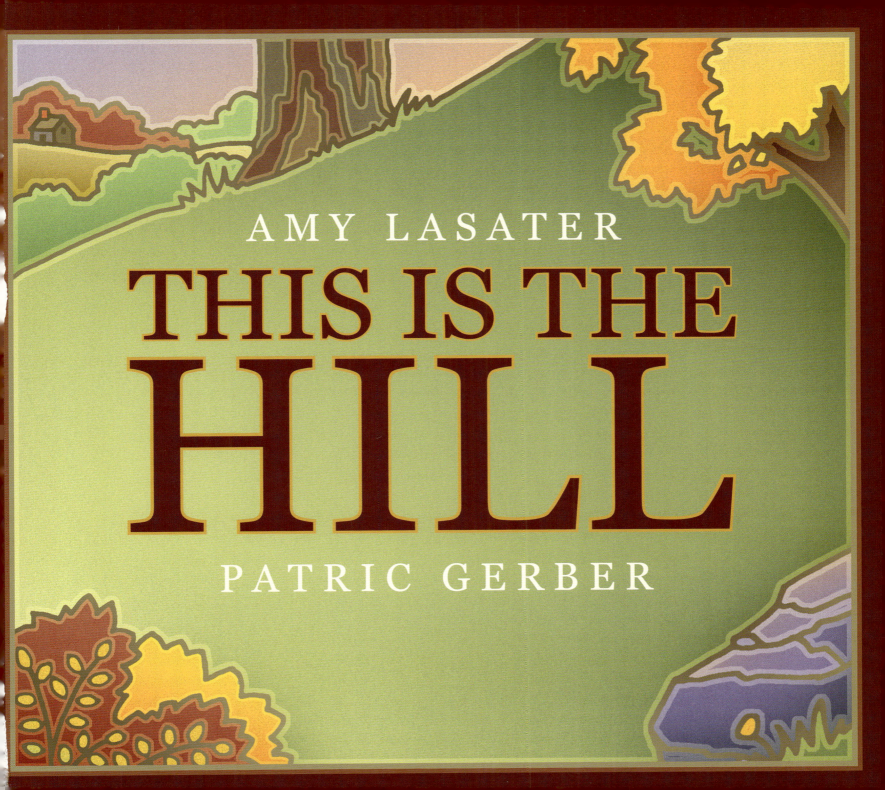

AMY LASATER

THIS IS THE HILL

PATRIC GERBER

For my husband, Garth,
and my children, Ashley, Christian, and Seth,
who have inspired me to share my testimony of the gospel.

—AMY LASATER

For my best collaborators and critics,
Suzan, Kennedy, Leslie, Sam, Owen, and Andrew.
—PATRIC GERBER

THIS IS THE HILL.

THIS IS THE HILL near Joseph's home.

THIS IS THE STONE, the sacred stone
that stands on the hill near Joseph's home.

THIS IS THE BOX that lies unknown,
hidden from everyone under the stone
that stands on the hill near Joseph's home.

THESE ARE THE PLATES
that were fashioned of gold,
that rest in the box that lies unknown,
hidden from everyone under the stone
that stands on the hill
near Joseph's home.

THIS IS THE ANGEL, Moroni of old,

who buried the plates that were fashioned of gold,

that rest in the box that lies unknown,

hidden from everyone under the stone

that stands on the hill near Joseph's home.

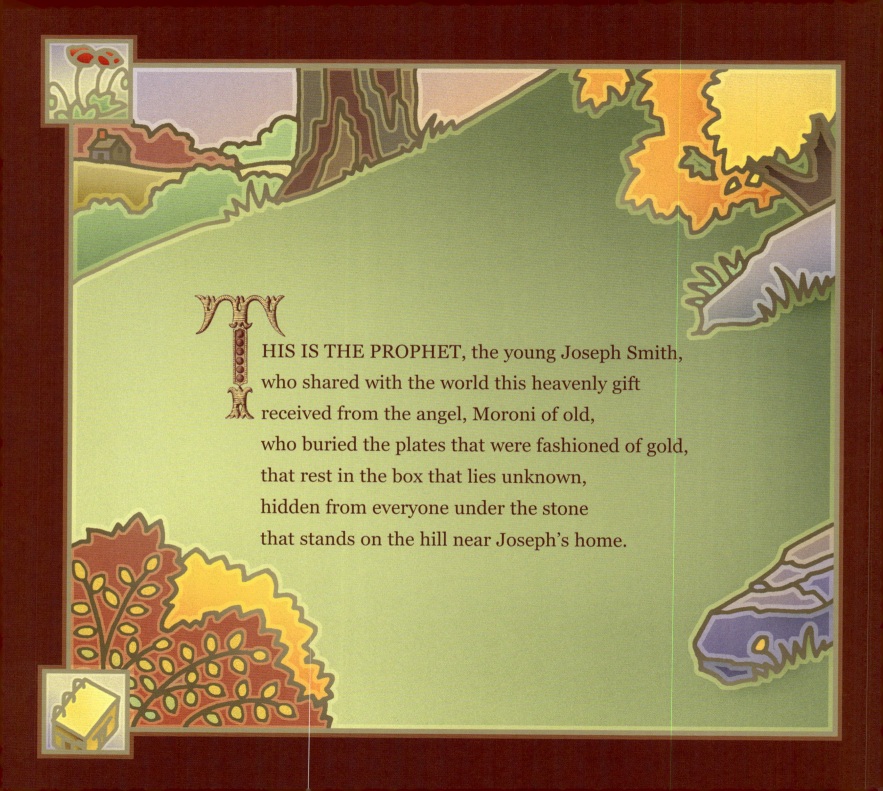

THIS IS THE PROPHET, the young Joseph Smith,
who shared with the world this heavenly gift
received from the angel, Moroni of old,
who buried the plates that were fashioned of gold,
that rest in the box that lies unknown,
hidden from everyone under the stone
that stands on the hill near Joseph's home.

THIS IS THE RECORD, the word of God,

the Book of Mormon, the iron rod,

translated by the young Joseph Smith,

who shared with the world this heavenly gift

received from the angel, Moroni of old,

who buried the plates that were fashioned of gold,

that rest in the box that lies unknown,

hidden from everyone under the stone

that stands on the hill near Joseph's home.

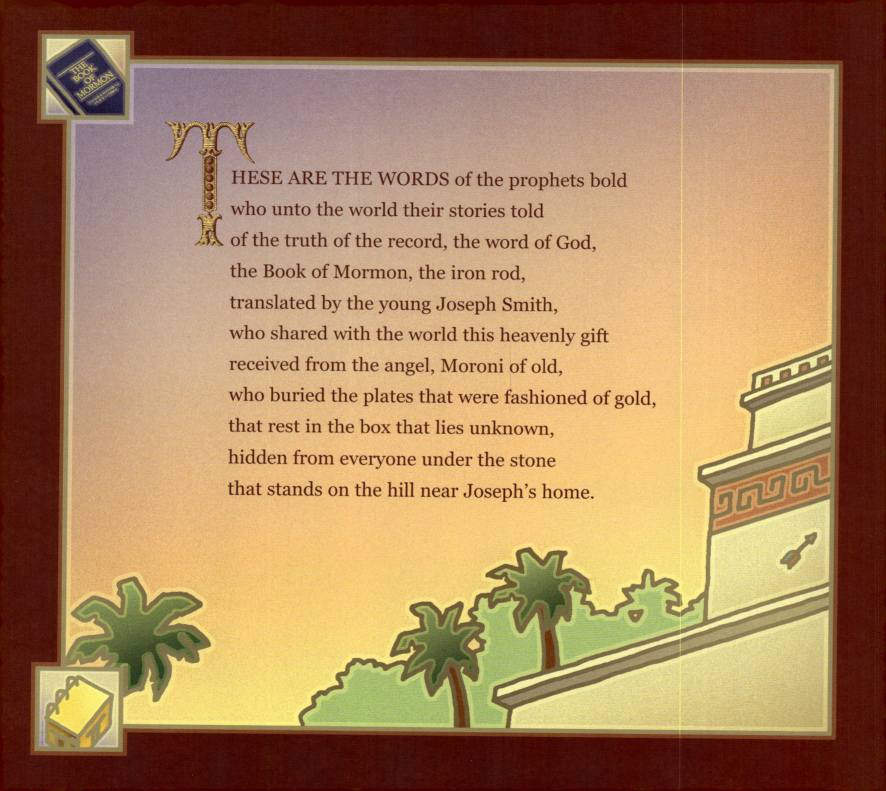

THESE ARE THE WORDS of the prophets bold
who unto the world their stories told
of the truth of the record, the word of God,
the Book of Mormon, the iron rod,
translated by the young Joseph Smith,
who shared with the world this heavenly gift
received from the angel, Moroni of old,
who buried the plates that were fashioned of gold,
that rest in the box that lies unknown,
hidden from everyone under the stone
that stands on the hill near Joseph's home.

THIS IS THE PROMISE that all should hear:
pray in faith—and be sincere—
that as you read, you'll know for sure
the truth of the words from the prophets bold
who unto the world their stories told
of the truth of the record, the word of God,
the Book of Mormon, the iron rod,
translated by the young Joseph Smith,
who shared with the world this heavenly gift
received from the angel, Moroni of old,
who buried the plates that were fashioned of gold,

that rest in the box that lies unknown,
hidden from everyone under the stone
that stands on the hill
near Joseph's home.

Published by Covenant Communications, Inc.
American Fork, Utah

Printed in China
First Printing: August 2005

11 10 09 08 07 06 05   10 9 8 7 6 5 4 3 2 1

ISBN 1-59156-720-3